THE PUGILIST'S DAUGHTER

poems by

Janet Lowery

Finishing Line Press
Georgetown, Kentucky

THE PUGILIST'S DAUGHTER

*Dedicated to the memory of my father,
Tim Lowery*

Copyright © 2020 by Janet Lowery
ISBN 978-1-64662-382-2 First Edition
All rights reserved under International and Pan-American Copyright Conventions. No part of this book may be reproduced in any manner whatsoever without written permission from the publisher, except in the case of brief quotations embodied in critical articles and reviews.

ACKNOWLEDGMENTS

"How Insomnia Runs Through a Bloodline" is forthcoming from *Texas in Poetry* 7, Texas Association of Creative Writing Teachers Conference (proceedings), San Angelo, September, 2020.
"My Father Falling" first appeared in *Concho River Review*, San Angelo, Spring 1994
"Married Off" first appeared as "Married" in *The California Quarterly*, Spring, 1991
"It Was Like This," "A Man Takes a Drink, A Drink Takes a Drink, A Drink Takes a Man.," and "I Never Said," were made public in the Mildred's Umbrella Theater Company's equity production of my play, *A Heroine-Free Summer*, Houston, spring 2017.

Publisher: Leah Maines
Editor: Christen Kincaid
Cover Art: Marie Lowery
Author Photo: Lela Anne Buvens
Cover Design: Elizabeth Maines McCleavy

Order online: www.finishinglinepress.com
also available on amazon.com

Author inquiries and mail orders:
Finishing Line Press
P. O. Box 1626
Georgetown, Kentucky 40324
U. S. A.

Table of Contents

How Insomnia Runs Through a Bloodline 1

Story 2

After My Seventh Christmas 6

First Night 7

Black Pearl 9

How It Played Out 10

What Could Have Stopped His Rants 12

Vigil 13

It Was Like This 14

That Way 15

Prayers 16

The Pugilist's Daughter 17

Greensfield Park, North Side, Age Thirteen 20

In My Father's Room 21

At Mass 22

Married Off 24

The Boxer 25

A Man Takes a Drink, A Drink Takes a Drink, A Drink Takes a Man 27

My Father Falling 29

I Never Said 30

Mourning Comes Electra 33

Karma 34

Childlike 35

How Insomnia Runs Through a Bloodline

If her father hadn't quit high school
at the age of seventeen and forged
his parents' signatures, first,
on the hospital forms for surgery
so his crossed-eye could be corrected,

and, second, on the enlistment papers
so he could sign-up though underage—
he would have missed World War II,
missed the Battle of the Bulge,
evaded battles that shattered

his vision, clouded his outlook,
caused suicidal urgings to haunt him
along with the ghosts of dead soldiers—
all the enemy men he shot, plus
his fallen comrades, and that one
fourteen year-old German soldier

who woke him from sleep every night
and kept him awake,
woke his children, too,
and kept them awake
for the rest of his life.
And for the rest of theirs.

Story

I.

There's no point in going back
to those dusty floorboards
near the two corner doors
into my mother's bedroom,
where her spot-lit daughter
still stands like a little soldier
at attention, like St. Joan
in armor before she took
command of the Dauphin's troops,
nervous and pacing in her heart,
her blood racing, her feet
standing in place, her hands
ready to take action,
pick up a sword or gun,
or push a big man down
with her bare hands.

No one needs to know
the story, the one that can't be true
the way she tells it.
Something was wrong, sure;
no one was in charge, no;
and everyone except her—
brother, sisters, mother—
kept screaming or crying
or hiding, while she watched,
waiting for her turn to strike.

II.

Meanwhile, at an invisible
window into another dimension,
the man playing her father
looks out at the backyard
with its swing set and rose bushes
one story below. He hides
behind a yellow drape
and weeps with his face
in his hands at the crime scene
going on behind his back,
the one he refuses to witness
unfolding in that room
where everyone except
his second daughter
points a finger at him—
or rather—at his doppelganger,
the man in a dark suit
who stands, weaving, drunk
in the midnight air.

He, the criminal, trespasses
in his own home. "I pay the bills,"
he thunders. Little sparks shoot out
into the grit of nighttime light;
red flames burst; miniature explosions
erupt from that other dimension
where the dread father lives—
at the German front
from that long ago forgotten war—

III.

Bullets whizz by in the air,
clots of dirt fly past,
men bleed out, their heads
cradled in his lap while
he keeps firing the 30-caliber
machine gun; the men's screams,
the blood in his lap, the cries
of young men dying in a foreign land—
that's the film running
behind his eyes.
And no escape, no one to turn to
and say "no—this is wrong,
something's wrong,
no one's in charge."

And he eighteen. And she,
nine, ten, eleven, twelve, thirteen—
eighteen, twenty-two—
and her brother and sisters,
still stuck in that room the way
he's still trapped in the mud
of that war—

He shot his children each night
with invisible guns
for the simple reason
that no one born from his seed
should live free if those men—
his comrades and so-called
enemies—had to die,
their bloodlines blotted out
while his marched on. No.

If he got to go home, marry,
and have children, then
all his offspring had to pay
the debt. It's the definition
of survivor guilt: who gets to
stay, who has to cross over
the great water. He shook
his head, black with tears.

IV.

None of his children
or his children's children
will enjoy the privilege
of walking around planet earth
feeling truly alive—none will
thrive, not if those men perished—
no. He blames himself.
Those who see action during war—
do they ever escape?

Guilt, like muck, is a heavy
weight one slogs through
or dives into as it sucks
one down into oblivion.
He drank until he was blind
and sought no man's land
between the living and the dead.

He closed his eyes
to his own actions after the war.
And who, other than his wife
and children, could blame him?

No one needs to know this story.

After My Seventh Christmas

I insisted my mother drive me to
a gift shop where an army of sainted
porcelain statuary stood on display
in anti-military formation.
Is it idolatry to surround oneself
with three dimensional images of
the angelic while living in the midst
of fear? An imaginative effort
to configure the sacred in clay, glaze,
and paint pays homage to the infinite,
but more to the point, I sought divine help.
I was six then seven then eight years old
and my family was fast falling apart.
What else could I do? I bought a rook of
angels, three china seraphs in pastel
colors. I bought a ceramic Mary
in blue robes, her foot crushing a fanged snake,
an Infant of Prague in satin cloth of gold,
an antique print of St. Joan I hung near
my bed—I insulated myself against
the plague-winds of domestic war in hopes
that, sleeping in an enemy camp, I'd
be sheltered by the supernatural.

First Night

I suffered my first earache one night
when I was nine—that cataclysmic year.
Acute pain—a lance—pierced the secret cells
of my inner ear, entered a pocket
of my fevered brain pan and nested there.
A few wayward tears leaked from my eyes;
I wished my father would come back home soon
and comfort me the way he always did
when I was sick. I couldn't sleep; I stared
at the light fixture above my sick bed:

Four circus characters etched in red
pirouetted around a circle of
blue frosted glass. I struggled to decide
which figure I liked best: the bald muscle-
man with the black mustache, the acrobat
standing on one satin toe, the sleek seal
balancing a ball on his nose-tip,
or the prancing pony with the red plume
and arched tail—but I couldn't decide—I
liked them all, I loved them all, they were so
happy. But the way my mother sighed as
she passed the door on her way downstairs,
her arms full of soiled laundry, bothered me.
And I didn't like waiting for my father.
It was after midnight.
                        Then he came home.
I heard his car in the drive and his steps
on the gravel and the side door slam shut
and his voice in the kitchen, then the stern
words my mother said to him. I worried
she'd drive him away when I wanted him
to come upstairs and visit me. Then up
she came, haughty and cold. Then he came up—

he had a heart of gold. He sat beside
me and whispered he loved me, he was sad
I was sick, I was his good little girl;
I wept with relief, but later, I knew.

His words slurred like syrup on a thick tongue.
His eyes looked like black glass buttons. I held
on tight and studied his face, hands, and breath,
I smelled the distilled fumes there. He rose on
unsteady feet to say goodnight, but lost
his balance and grabbed onto the wall.

When he left the room, he was gone forever.
I asked if he was an alcoholic,
and when my mother nodded with contempt,
I went blind with fury. I plotted how
I would cure my father's affliction and
prove to my mother he was a good man—
and that I—I was a good man's daughter.

Black Pearl

My father was habitual with drink,
but I'd made a fool's pact with the divine.
I was nine when I mustered the courage
one night to ask my father—trembling—to
stop drinking. He leaned back, shuffled his feet,
shook his head no, and laughed. I crumbled at
the knees, swooned to the bottom bunk, and cried
like the nine year old child I was.
      My mother slipped a tranquilizer in
my mouth to shut me up and held onto
my sister, but I wept until grief took
me down to the mouth of a rolling river
that opened on a world absent love or
joy or hope—a nickel-gray sea across
which a large round pewter-black pearl floated
toward the horizon line deep down inside
my hallucination of mortal woe.
      On gray waves in my imagination,
the pearl bobbed repeatedly, pointlessly,
stupidly to say: *This is it. The end.*
Get over it. Nothing means anything.
Your ideas about God and goodness
are fantastical, egotistical
fool's gold. How difficult it is to survive
a wearying childhood. How mighty is
the child who overpowers a grim past.

How It Played Out

After a while my father didn't go
to my mother's bedroom anymore, no,
he came to mine. It wasn't that he touched
me—he wasn't depraved like her brothers—
he was merely another black-out drunk
looking for attention. I was the child
he'd three times rescued from death's dark threshold,
a daddy's girl living in a fool's paradise
with a drunk and willful father to whom
she owed her young life. Late at night, he feared
the ghost of that boy soldier he'd shot dead
on the frontlines might return from the dead
and he'd be forced to shoot or get shot
one more time, so he leaned on the top bunk
and talked to me like I was an adult.

We debated Catholic theology—
whether or not he'd go to hell. Worried sick
his drinking would land him in flames,
I'd figure out how to save him from that fate
when the time came, but just then it was
my grammar school catechism versus
his Jesuit training; I always lost,
but, dizzy with the attention, I got
drunk on my newly elevated status
as his confessor and closest confidant.

I didn't want him to go see my mother
anyways. I didn't like her. It was
a sin, but I had thrown in with him, we
were in cahoots against my poor, troubled,
long-suffering mother—whose own mother
was doubly unkind—she just couldn't win—
my mother—but for me, it was Electra
all over again—bitter against her
mother, too fond of her wayward father—
how could a child thrive with such a dire fate?
But I was born of good cheer; my dad taught
me to laugh at a cruel destiny, so later on,
when I found a way to dig my way out
of the underworld's gloom, I dug like hell.

Who Could Have Stopped His Rants

They say someone else—
one of his brothers or his father—
should have set him straight,
a friend, maybe, a business partner,
the Chief of Police in that tiny hometown—
he was the man her father drank with
every night at the Blue Haven—
or one of his wife's brothers—though
none was a match for a former boxer
in the U.S. Army with an IQ of 160,
a former gunner on the front lines—
They say it should have been anyone
other than her at the age of nine
ten, eleven, twelve, etc.,—but it wasn't.
That's the way the cookie crumbles.

Vigil

I watched for my father to trip then fall and hit his head
in a drunken stumble up the hill to our house,
an aura of death emanating from him—veteran
of foreign wars that he was, an infantry man,
a gunner on the German front lines, a soldier
still carrying over his shoulders on memory's
battlefield the barely visible forms of fallen friends,
still talking it over in his intoxicated brain—
how this bullet or that shell caught his young buddy
in the skull or the eye, how if he'd leaned this way
or that, swung the thirty-caliber machine gun left or right,
maybe the boys he loved would have survived.

It became his mission: saving comrades
who'd already died, discussing with the ghosts
he carried over his shoulders or the ones limping
at his side how on earth they could have departed
for eternity without him, why their bleeding heads
fell into his lap instead of his into theirs, and why
they'd tried to slip into nirvana without him, leaving
his soul to rot on earth among the miserable living.
And it became my mission to save my father
from the miasma of war, the fantasy playing out
in his intoxicated struggle up the hill.

I gently slid one of the soldiers from my father's back
and lifted him over my own young shoulders.
Months later I took on another, and another,
and in this way, I came to prop up on my own back
a few ghosts of WWII, I shouldered the fighters
through the daylight hours and rested with them
into twilight, watched the sun set on yet another day
in a world they didn't know how to leave, stayed
with them down the long tunnel of night as they
stuck with me when I knocked my far-gone-father
to the ground each night with their affectionate help,
none of us remembering how or why fallen soldiers
came to be my wards, the only ones I've ever helped,
the ones I eased off one day to the far shore of hope,
freeing us all of war's catastrophic burden.

It Was Like This:

My older sister stood on my right, whining and screaming,
her blue eyes red, her small mouth contorted with hatred
for my father and me. She hit or scratched or cursed me
when I told her to shut up, my heart already black,
closed down with contempt so thick it fit like taut muscles
over the bare bones of my body. And my mother on my left
sat forward on her bed, the white sheets and chenille spread
thrown to her waist, her pleas or demands unheeded by my father
who stood in the center of the room, weaving in the night air
as he pulled the light chord on and off and on and off,
taunting us as we scrambled to outwit his drunken heart.

Across the hallway my younger brother hid in his bed,
ashamed. And in the doorway my younger sisters stood—
tearful, fretful. They waited for someone smart to save them,
but it would not be me. When my temper finally broke
and I bit the night in two, when I stepped up to my father,
raised my hands into the reeling air and pushed hard on his chest,

when I finally knocked my father down, watched his feet
skid on the hardwood floor, his hands grapple
with the slippery air, his body crash into a bedpost, a dresser
on his slow heartbreaking descent to the floor,
when I saw him lie there on his broad back
like a stunned animal and hiss each breath at the ceiling,
his eyes small glints of light blinking in the darkness,
that's when I'd crouch on the floor and weep.
I rubbed tears into the cracks between floorboards
and listened to my mother whisk the other girls off to bed
with a hush and a kiss. My father whispered
into the ragged mouth of night he'd never forgive me for this.

That Way

None of his children pronounced the word "drunk"
to describe their father's state of being.
No. When he came home on a random eve,
they asked each other if he was *that way*.
Solemn nods. Home for dinner, he'd stroll back
out the side door afterwards, stumble down Main
until he hit the Blue Haven. Brick glass
framed a large window tinted black. She looked
inside once to see human silhouettes
propped atop barstools, a vignette from hell
inhabited by trolls and rumpled vets.
Cool blue neon and golden light crisscrossed
a sleek bar where the seeds of her father's
doom—planted years before—bloomed.

Prayers

Her older sister prayed to a god the girl knew not of:
please let him get arrested and sent to prison.

Please let him go to jail for ten years or kill
himself in a car wreck where no one else is hurt,

hit a telephone pole, crack his head
open and bleed out, please let him drive

off a cliff never to be seen or heard from again,
please let Mom divorce him or her kick him out.

Meanwhile the girl fretted about him daily:
would he ever come home sober again,

would he even come home at all, would he get
in a car wreck and die, would he fall down

and cut himself, would he lose his job and slip
back into depression and kill himself?

She begged him to divorce her mother or just give
her one good reason why he had married the woman.

The one time the mom called the cops, they came
to the door and said, "Hi, Tim," then told her mother

she had to leave while her drunk husband got to stay;
his name was on the deed, though *her* mother

made the down payment. So Mom packed a suitcase
and went to her mother's for the night. All the kids cried.

Even the girl, who loved her father and considered
her mother an enemy, knew the cops were dead wrong.

The Pugilist's Daughter

My father was a pugilist, a welter-weight boxer
during World War II, a womanizer, an Irish scrapper—
god—how the Irish love to fight. Is it from centuries
of poverty and British oppression? Is that where
we get our spunk? Or is it the barbarian inside us,
the naked, warp-spasmed, shape-shifting Celts,
so feared on the field of battle the Romans
declined to conquer us? My father—a perfect example—
could size up a man with one intoxicated blink
and cut him in half with a word. When he was drunk—
which was almost every night—he dominated
my sisters and brother, he ruthlessly humiliated
my mother, beat her down, beat his kids down with words—
never with fists—always with mocking words.

But never me. Nope. Never me. I was his favorite,
the fool of the household. When he was sober
I deliberated with him point by point on punishments
he doled out, then passed judgment on his decisions.
But when he was drunk and on a tear, I listened
and watched, I took notes: his arrogant sneers,
his insolent disregard for others caused me
insufferable shame—my once-upon-a-time hero
was an ethical disaster. But he was an expert
at verbal jabs. His tight arguments lashed out
with the swift logic of his one-two punch;
he threw a brilliant philosophical left hook—
even in a blacked-out blind drunk.

Then the instant came when I said, *enough*.
Standing in the doorway of my bedroom one night—
where most hung-over mornings he blessed my sister
and me in Latin—he leaned against the door frame,
too intoxicated to stand. I stepped up to the plate
and made my plea: for the sake of all, he should give it up,

his love affair with alcohol. I had common sense on my side:
he was causing trouble. Didn't we often discuss conduct?
Virtue? Discipline? Heaven? He laughed my request
into the gutter of ill-repute. While I stood in the middle
of my bedroom floor like a little soldier, he played the tough
with me, his daughter, he performed the scorn-filled hero
defending his platform of privilege to a desperate child.
That was it. The door to my regard banged shut.

One week later, during his stint as master of ceremonies
in our routine midnight circus, under the spotlight
of a bare bulb in my mother's room, my cold-hearted
cynicism got the best of me and I knocked
him down, the one who knocked everyone else down.
From his six-foot, two-hundred-and-twenty-pound
pedestal of drunken male power I pushed him
with all my might and he fell, slamming a path
through every proximate piece of furniture
on his way to the floor. He fell like the animal
he was. I was nine years old. A stiff wind
could have knocked him over, but that wasn't what
the fates had arranged. Nope. It was me against him,
me against him for months, years, on and off
until I was twenty-two. One of my younger sisters
took over the battle when I went away to college.

She hated his guts, but for me, he'd been my favorite
parent, by far more beloved than my mother—
that weak vain money-grubbing victim.
My contempt for her at that time was a futile curse,
my allegiance to my father a conflict within my heart
eternally burning. For he was a great story teller,
a good poker player, a quick-witted practical joker;
he always took the role of Captain Hook
when we played Peter Pan on his big double bed,

he scared us into giggles with his crimped-hand
pawing the air to capture us—the lost boys or the tribe
of orphaned Indians led by the clever fearless Tiger Lily.

Still, today, I wander the world like a lost child,
an Indian girl. For twelve brutal adolescent years
I led the gang of rebels in our house, I found
the outrage in my heart that fuels courage,
I protected my mother and the others from him.
That job hung around my neck like a jeweled albatross.
I used to come out of a corner swinging with all
my might at perceived bullies, my shoulders and arms,
my entire chest so fortified by fear and a distorted
desire for justice, I knocked about like a wayward child
for years. How painful it is to be a woman who was a girl
raised to push her father to the ground. The Fighting Irish.
God Bless us as we tear each other down.

Greensfield Park, North Side, Age Thirteen

Clouds drifted the sky that summer day in
small-town, upstate New York. Flat on the grass,
I stared up until I slept then woke then felt
the ground beneath my back clasp onto me
to hold my form the way a mother holds
a child. I leaned into the earth. Shivers
shot up and down my spine. The sky's grace fell
into my eye invisibly and then
everything in the universe shifted
into place.   All gloom and adolescent
despair evaporated into air.
I flattened more against the earth's broad back,
my eyes fixed on the spectacle of sky
as if I'd never seen that blue before.
I held my breath, I held the ground; I think
I heard inside my ears my heart pound out
its steady living sound. I knew what was
happening: I'd come into disbelief
and I was not meant to live in disbelief.

So now the infinite pulsed through me
a message, a reminder about our
deal, our pact, my place, its power—and so
a calm came over me, a relief and
peace, the kind *that passeth all understanding.*
The sun warmed my face. The grass cooled my skin.
The good earth held me in her *cradle rocking.*
A sensibility beneath and above
included me in its counting. My doubt
fled in the face of that rich harmony,
and—blessed that day—I accepted the blessing.

In My Father's Room

My father's room was as neat as a pin.
Still my mother called me up from a book
and took me by the hand with her to look
for dirt inside his sanctuary. As in
a dream, she mopped beneath his bed. Back,
and forth she swished, then wiped a cloth between
his nightstand lamp and the *Time* magazines
he often studied in bed, his thick black
glasses propped on his nose as he reclined
against a pillow. I knew something was
up before she rifled through a few mussed-
up issues and revealed her precious find:
a magazine called *Playboy*. She flipped
it open and displayed shiny pictures
of women from circus acts or outer
space, their enormous breasts grotesque, their lips
puckered, pouting and pink, their cheeks rouged red,
their underlined eyes bright and dead as glass.

My mother had struck a deathblow. But as
if the cut were not deep enough, she said:
*Why would any women do such a thing
as this?* And I was nine years old. *Why would
your father buy these magazines?* And I
wanted to kill her. Mumbling something, I
left to fume in *blue uncertain* rage inside
my room, doomed to wander there, lost and
mad bewildered. I turned to the dresser
where my china angels stood arranged, less
the one who'd fallen and broken a wing.
How like her I was. She lay wounded in
a secret drawer waiting to be made whole.
I glued her wing back on, affixed soul to
socket to free her from earth once again.

At Mass

My father, hung over, his breath reeking
of drink, wobbles in the besotted suit
of his affliction. He rocks his wingtips
from toe to heel unconsciously; his gut
bumps to and fro with inebriated
irregular beats against the waxed rim
of the pew-back at ten thirty Mass on
Sundays at St James, pre-Vatican II.

Mass is in Latin—the dark sonorous
language my father studied throughout
parochial grammar school, and later,
as an altar boy in the good old days
before World War II, when, still a tough kid
at the Christian Brothers Academy,
he cut confession lines, fist-fought the Brothers
who taught him how to box after they chased
him down side streets for the misdemeanor.

I stand next to him—his staunch protector
and defender—despite his height and weight,
despite the scent of booze and cigarettes
befouling the air; despite my fear that he
might soon lose his balance, topple over,
or fall asleep standing straight up;
despite the smudged and scorched air circling
his whiskey-saturated frame, despite
possible humiliation and shame

for his condition. If kind Fr. Browne's
homily goes long—as it sometimes does—
my father gives a knowing, patient wink.
If cold Fr. Dirk's homily turns cruel—
as is the norm—my father rolls his eyes
and cracks a conspiratorial smile

that says we'll suffer his mean speech but it
won't bring us down, no, it won't kill our fun.
He suppresses a guffaw, I swallow
a laugh, then he gives me a warning glance
re: my super-serious stern mother,
his insufferable wife. We straighten up
to avoid one of her withering looks.

I study the flock of white and gold angels
circling the blue dome of the church,
or stare at panes of cobalt blue, red, green,
and gold stained-glass windows lining the walls.
Sometimes it's the twinkle and flicker of
candlelight, sometimes the sculpted angels,
the mosaic tile, or painted plaster-work
that distracts me from our family drama,

but since the night I played the God-card and
lost, it's turned serious. I'm ten years old.
When I shut my eyes, I will myself dead
and gone, yet when they flutter open, pain
dissolves in a blue votive flame. The curve of
an angel's wing transports me back to worlds
so full of grace, my racked spirit brightens.
All will be well someday say the angels.
Against my better judgment, I believe.

Married Off

So he came to me at night, leaned on the top bunk
and talked like I was a grown-up, a confidant,
a wife. My sister on the bottom bunk fussed, but
he told her to go straight to hell, he was so cruel—
we called him the Big D when he wasn't around.
He looked like Jackie Gleason, Johnny Cash, and James
Garner, his dark hair so thick and black, he had to
push it off his forehead with his big Irish hands.
Oh, he was handsome, his mouth a mere line, his eyes
small and bright black, his brows dark and expressive.
I never tired of watching him, I studied him
until I became him, my father as a young girl.

So this was my disease: my father and I merged,
our fates blended and everyone knew it, they left us
alone to talk in the dark, one of us standing
next to the top bunk, the other sitting up, pitched
forward, listening to the other ramble on. And
he never told me to go straight to hell, and I
never told him to leave the room, I didn't
want him to go to my mother—she was heartless,
she'd turn him away, wound him again, and I'd
never do that, I knew he was helpless, a child,
already broken from booze. Where was
his mother, I wondered, and did she love him?

He'd had a crossed eye until age seventeen, is
that what ruined him? Or was it the war he joined
as a boy, his friends blown up beside him? Why had
my mother turned her back on him, and then on me?
He was the drunken husband she'd come to despise,
whereas I longed to heal him of his disease and
go back to being a kid full-time, racing down
the length of Crocker Avenue, outrunning boys
and dogs, leaping sidewalk cracks and roots of trees
without a care in the world—those years before
it came to pass I was married off to my father
by my mother. Long before the sins of the father
passed down to the daughter who loved him most.

The Boxer

My father threw a swing at me one night
in the half-dark of my mother's bedroom.
He told me how he stood in a perfect
boxer's stance the night he landed a punch
on the jaw of the Italian owner
of a gas station outside Rochester,
into whose gas pump my drunken father's
car had veered, knocking it askew. "What's wrong
with you?" the man yelled. My father climbed
out of the car and studied the error of his ways.

An insurance claims adjuster back then,
he knew the guy's policy would cover
the damage, but the fiery man threw
a fist at my father and missed.
My dad knocked him out with one punch.

Whenever he told the story, he'd shrug
and roll his eyes as if to say, "What could I do?"
When my father drove off, the man regained
consciousness and phoned the state troopers.
They turned their sirens on and chased my father
down Route 31, north of the New York
State Thruway towards Syracuse, but my dad
eluded them, he gunned the car and blew
through barricades. Then troopers opened fire
and hit his car. And it was a company car.

With nine counts against him, my dad
stood before a judge who knew him well from
insurance claims court. The judge liked my dad,
everybody liked my dad, the judge said
the only way to beat the rap was to get
everyone to drop the charges. And so,
full of charming remorse, my father told
and re-told the story of how a bartender

at his favorite saloon had concocted
an experimental drink and plied him
with its sly poisons on that ill-fated night;
its adverse effects had pushed his crazy actions—
he wasn't really like that, no, he was
a husband, a father, a veteran of World

War II, a graduate of Le Moyne University,
a devout Catholic. The troopers bought it
and dropped the charges. The Italian guy agreed
to drop all but one. That's when my father
pulled out his ace card; that's when he said to
the man, "Don't do it for me, do it for my kids."

What could the poor guy do? It was the fifties.
He forgave all the charges. Blind with drink,
my father threw a fake sucker punch my way
one scary night when I was twelve years old.
I refused to flinch, but my world collapsed.
I didn't know what I was supposed to do
with the fear that blew like a storm in and out
of the hole my father's fist had made
when it rushed like a black wind past my eyes,
so close I carried it with me for years, like a sad story
I never wanted to tell—one with a twist at the end
that's unfamiliar, but not quite a surprise.

A Man Takes a Drink, A Drink Takes a Drink, A Drink Takes a Man

I remember the dead-weight way my father lay
on a mattress on the floor in the closet-sized room
when he stayed with me for a few months in 1977
between bouts of chronic alcoholism and bouts
of manic depression; when he hid in my apartment
so he could dry out, pretend to quit drinking again
and rest inside the womb of my love as if
it were a cocoon out of which he could metamorphose
into a magical being imbued with wings of light.

Most mornings, he could not rise from the mattress,
could not pull himself upright, he could barely
roll over to face me, his daughter, squatting near
the bed, talking in a low voice to ask him
how was he doing, what was wrong, what could I do
to help? The worst mornings his voice broke,
he'd cover his handsome face with his big Irish hands
and half-sob a few clotted tears, his barrel chest
convulsing beneath the T-shirt he wore as pajama tops.
I'd pat his arm or back, smooth a cotton sleeve,

I'd cry too, the air above our heads saturated with gloom.
I didn't like to watch my father die in slow stages
from the guilt of soldiering, I didn't want to see him
collapse mentally only to rise again months later
in a frenzied upswing, ready to rock and roll,
ready to hit the streets, drink again with money
he'd saved while living off me, money the government
gave him because he'd lost his job, spent his savings
on booze, sold his credit cards, cheated the IRS,
smuggled cocaine over the Mexican border,
hit the skids, and landed in the Salvation Army
in Brownsville, Texas.

Years later, in a bar, still at it, he'd tell me "Drinking is
the thinking man's addiction," as if that explained it all,
but just then, I didn't like to see my father sob into his hands—
I could barely stand the crack and groan of his words.
Still, it was my fate to witness his heavy fall and so,
I'd crouch there on the floor and watch light glint off tears
caught in his eyes, I'd watch his body shake and I'd feel
my body shake too, I'd feel my sense of self crash
and slide—so intent was I on rescuing my father,
I could not see myself inside the wide regions of my brain.

And though he would disappear again in a matter of weeks
and I wouldn't see his rugged face or hear his soulful voice
for three long years, I waited it out, this suffering.
I dug my heels into the hardwood floor and rocked forward
to comfort my father as he wept, all the electrons swirling
above our heads in one genetic maelstrom of despair.

My Father Falling

So if each night before I fall asleep,
I raise my dead father from his grave,
dress him again in his print pajamas,
if I wake him up to put him back to bed
to watch him rise the last night of his life,
the night the electric pain shot through
his chest in a black vine of disbelief
and he sat-up, threw off the covers and lurched
into the dark air clutching his heart;

if I keep raising my father from the dead
to put him through this routine over and over
in slow motion so I can study his expression
and note whether a flicker of larger awareness
hammered its silver nail into his head
so that he knew too late, but still he knew,
that this was it—his last breath, his last
vision of the world: the blue bed covers,
his second wife's stupid helpless face,

the knowledge that no, he would not
gather his children one last day around
his shabby table to dole out final words
of regret and apology; if I keep
reviewing his struggle to make it
into the bathroom where the nitro tablets
sit waiting in their amber pill bottle
rather than on the night stand
next to his bed, thinking: if the nitro

had been on the night stand, why would he
have to get up, why in fact did he have to
wake up at all? Why didn't he die in his sleep
like my evil grandmother? But, of course,
he was too smart to miss the excitement
of his own death.

                          If I keep watching
his hands in the dark, trying to imagine
his head hitting the floor, the exact position
of his body—was he face down, on his side,
or flat on his back, staring up blankly
at the vanishing ceiling, or did he bang his head
on the way down—while his fall keeps

happening in my mind over and over again,
slowly, my eye like a camera isolating his thick
black hair, his flushed cheeks, his black eyes
like beads of light, his thin mouth, red hands,
the slope of his belly, his thin hips, white legs,
muscular calves, his long, flat white feet.

If I keep watching my father drop to his death
each night, both love and relief lulling me
to sleep, if I do this exercise, this meditation,
if I repeat this prayer over and over, slowing
his fall, actually breaking his fall, cradling
his head in my invisible arms before it hits
the carpet, will I let myself live in peace,
will I forgive myself for not being there
to catch him, not being there to say goodbye?

I Never Said

I never said what it was like to be your kid
when I was your kid. I could hardly stutter,
my heart jammed so far up my throat,
I swallowed words I longed to cast
to magical effect on all those dwelling inside
the household at 24 Second Street, a street
where quiet distress echoed from my mother's
retreat in the add-on's spare back bedroom,
just off the bedroom I shared with my sister.

I never mentioned how the sound
of your station wagon pulling into the drive
at night clenched my hands around the sheets,
churned my guts to knots, I never said
how my teeth tore my nails in the dark,
gnawed the skin off raw cuticles. Trapped
on that top bunk, I felt the ceiling press
down on my brains, my wits flatten
with despair. You never struck anyone
those nights—I was the violent one—
the one to act—the one who loved you.

Still, I never said how once your foot hit
the stairs my body stiffened; once your weight
popped the handrail from its metal socket,
I held the fear down by its arms
and legs like a fitful child struggling
to break free from the frame of fate choking
the life out of her nine-year old lungs.

I never explained how self-pity gathered
in pools behind my face. I never told you
how scared I was when you argued
at two a.m. for the upper hand—your red mouth
roaring like the drunk you were, scorning
my mother's sniveling martyrdom to
a cause she'd stopped believing in.

It was an old battle from lifetimes ago,
but I couldn't know that when I was a kid
standing between you two, a witness,
a peacekeeper, and constable. I never said
the endless repetition was killing me—
how each night the same scenes, the same lines,
the same moans and gestures of defiance
numbed me to contempt, how I came to feel
older and wiser and stronger than both of you.

I never mentioned how I dreamed
of pulling the masks off your faces to insist
you both act like real parents; how I waited
for years to be told the whole family drama
was a trick of fantasy designed to teach me some
cathartic lesson, and now that I had memorized

all the lines, the black comedy called childhood
could shut down, pull up stakes, and leave town,
forever. And now that you've passed on
into the next world, I'm hoping you'll make good
from the other side of the veil, dispel all your
grief and gloom to the high heavens and let me go—
as befitting your happier station in the afterlife.

Mourning Comes Electra

Where is my father now, now that he is dead?
Is he down south in Brownsville, Texas, in bed
with a Mexican woman in a cheap hotel,
drinking whiskey from a bottle, resigned to hell?

Or is he walking down a hallway in our Second
Street house, the upstairs mirror blackened
with watery shadows spirited from the corners
of his saturated mind?
                        Is he walking forlorn
up the hill we lived on, stumbling so vaguely
only his children spot the slur in his sagging
steps, the blur in the gaze of his small black eyes?

Is he sitting in his favorite chair, loosening his tie,
his suit disheveled, his thoughts stupefied?
Is he sleeping alone on his big double bed or
on the banks of the Susquehanna, the shores
of the Rio Grande?
                        Where is my father now,
now that he's dead? And when he gets out
of hell this time, will he be better off
than the time before? Will he take comfort
from life in the afterlife? Where does he sleep at night,
and is his sleep sound; does he dream he shrugs off
the haunting shadows, the ghosts, the chills?

Is he asleep on a bed of rocks or a bed of silk?
Is he doing penance for his shame, roiling in guilt,
or has he risen above the pain of the war he carried
with him everywhere he stepped.
                        I hope he remembers my hands
and feet, the way I laughed at his jokes when I was young.
I don't want him to suffer there as much as he suffered
here on earth. I want him to make good,
somehow, on the other side of the grave.

Karma

I'm moving away from my father now,
swimming past his night blindness—
my blind eye, blinking with salt, with loss.

I wanted to see halfway, the way he saw,
I wanted to lift the weight of war
off his shoulders and carry it for him

like a backpack I slung over my shoulders
when I hitchhiked cross-country, back
in the old days of youthful adventure.

But now I'm swimming away instead,
swimming upstream toward the mouth of water,
swimming slow and awkward, my pale body

shivering in the emerald light of the lake,
flashing white as a silver fish, my torso
tossing and turning, drops of water streaming

my cheeks clean, long hair flowing wild,
water running through cupped fingers,
my feet kicking and splashing as I wriggle from

the straitjacket I'd strapped myself into
when a child. How hard it is to shed one layer
of skin, to throw off the weight of my father,

abandon his hands, his voice, the skew
of his eyesight. How difficult it is to swim
like a fish, one eye full of light,

the other eye dark as the murky bottom,
the top of my body shimmering like the moon,
the underside crossed with shadows.

Child-like

When I was ten years old, I believed in words
the way a child believes in prayer. I knelt
on the cold floor beside my bed, hands clasped,
repeating a plea before I leapt under the covers
to hide. When that plan didn't work, I came
to believe a magic phrase floated in the universe
above my awareness that would do the trick:
I'd formulate a prayer that actually worked,
a hymn of praise or gratitude that won favor,
I'd learn an incantation or a turn a rhyme
in a plough-line of verse that served
the mystical purpose I'd undertaken:
neutralize the discordant elements in the fabric
of my father's soul and reset his life's path away
from chronic addiction to alcohol.

With severe focus, a sleuth on the hunt
for clues to an obscure family murder,
I scrutinized page after page, passage after passage,
I hunted word after word with a fully lit brain
for the silver key, the single quintessential yes
to my father's absolute universal no, the golden
equation, the sacred frequency—I sought
the perfect tiny instrument I'd use to perform
psychic surgery—as if by sounding the words,
I'd cancel out the knell of doom spreading
through my family like a dissonant cloud
and replace it with a chord of harmony, a spell,
a chant that once spoken aloud could
deliver to all hearers a state of consciousness
akin to that winged thing I'd read about in a poem.

So, when I found those words, I repeated them
like a child kneeling beside a bed, one who
stitches up the seams of her own soul
with a silver needle and golden thread,
one who witnesses the wounds sewn shut,
the scars dissolved into precious patterns
in her soul like water-marked silk and then
whispers: it is done. And so it is. Amen.

www.ingramcontent.com/pod-product-compliance
Lightning Source LLC
LaVergne TN
LVHW041558070426
835507LV00011B/1160